By Shelly Neilsen
Illustrated by Anastasia Mitchell

Published by Abdo & Daughters, 4940 Viking Drive Suite 622, Edina, Minnesota 55435.

Library bound edition distributed by Rockbottom Books, Pentagon Tower, P.O. Box 36036, Minneapolis, Minnesota 55435.

**Edited by Julie Berg**

**LIBRARY OF CONGRESS CATALOGING-IN-PUBLICATION DATA**

Nielsen, Shelly. 1958 -
    I love air / written by Shelly Neilsen
        p.   cm. -- (Target Earth)
    Summary: Brief text and suggested activities introduce air and the good things it provides.
    ISBN 1-56239-189-5
    1. Air -- Juvenile literature. 2. Air -- Experiments -- Juvenile literature.
[1. Air.] 2. Pets.] I. Title. II. Series.
    QC161.N54  1993
    533 .6--dc20
    [B]                                          93-7597
                                                  CIP
                                                  AC

 Thanks To The Trees From Which This Recycled Paper Was First Made.

# I LOVE AIR PLEDGE

I promise to love the air. I'll let it blow and tangle my hair. I'll let it carry my imagination far, far away. I'm glad I'm a kid who loves the air.

Everyone needs air to breathe—clean, clean air!

I breathe in.  Out.  In.  Out.  I love air.

Can you hold your breath? Not for long! How many times do you breathe in one minute? People need air to live. Take a deep breath. You deserve it!

I love air. Air blows fluffy dandelion seeds far away. Blow, wind, blow. Carry the seeds to a new home. Grow, seeds, grow. I love air.

I LOVE AIR

IDEA BOX

Find two downy feathers. Play this game with a friend. Let the wind carry your feathers away. Whose feather floats the farthest?

I love air.  In the summer, the air is warmed by the sun. It feels good on my skin.  Sometimes summer air smells like coconut suntan oil and flowers.  I love air.

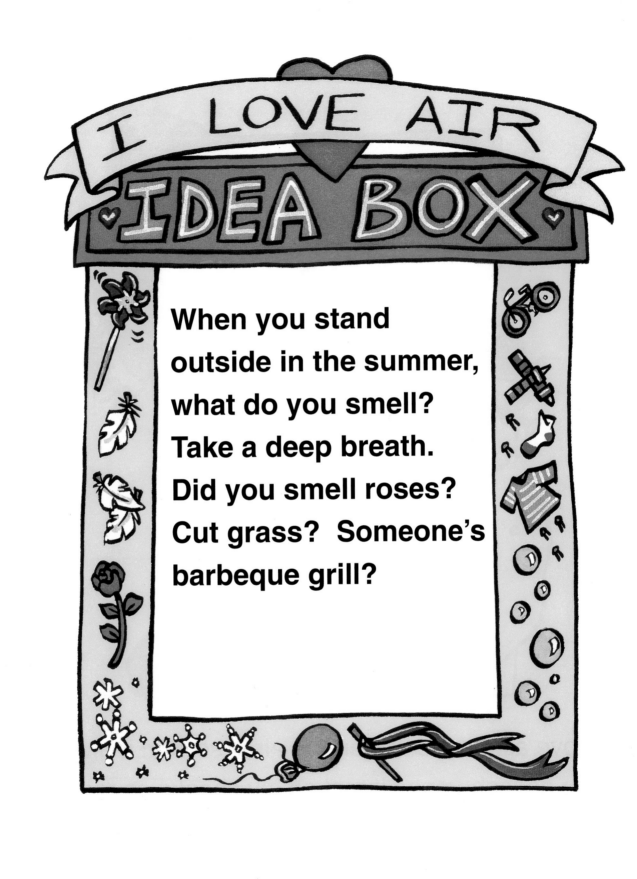

# I LOVE AIR

## IDEA BOX

When you stand outside in the summer, what do you smell? Take a deep breath. Did you smell roses? Cut grass? Someone's barbeque grill?

I love air.  In the winter, the air is so cold it gives me goosebumps.  It makes my cheeks as red as my mittens.  Winter air smells good—like clean icicles and snow.  I love air.

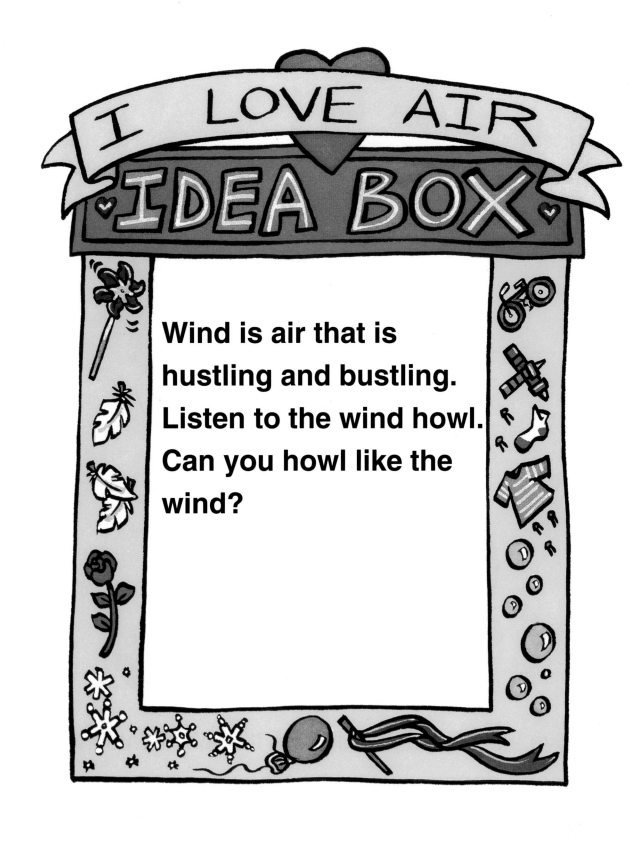

# I LOVE AIR

## IDEA BOX

Wind is air that is hustling and bustling. Listen to the wind howl. Can you howl like the wind?

I love air.  My balloon flies in the air.   Watch it
dip and dance.  Without air, how would balloons
fly?  I love air.

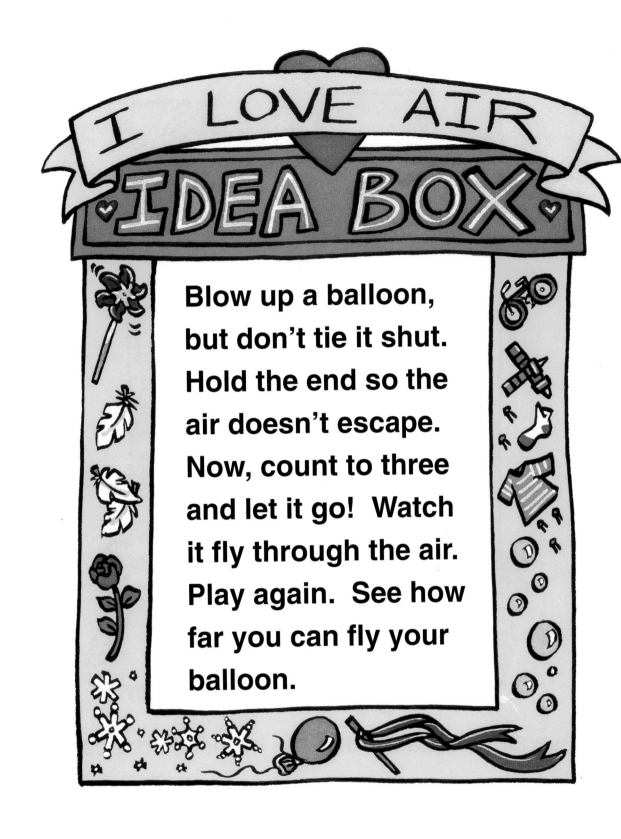

# I LOVE AIR

## IDEA BOX

Blow up a balloon, but don't tie it shut. Hold the end so the air doesn't escape. Now, count to three and let it go! Watch it fly through the air. Play again. See how far you can fly your balloon.

I love air. Air makes the tree branches dance. It tickles the grass. It ruffles my cat's hair—and mine, too. I love air.

# I LOVE AIR

## IDEA BOX

Make a wind stick from a long, straight pole or branch. Tape colorful ribbon or crepe paper to the top. Push the stick into the ground. Which way do the strips move? They tell you which way the wind is blowing.

I love air.  In the swimming pool, I hold tight to my air mattress.  The wind pushes me here and there.  I pretend I'm a sea-riding sailor.  Ahoy!  I love air.

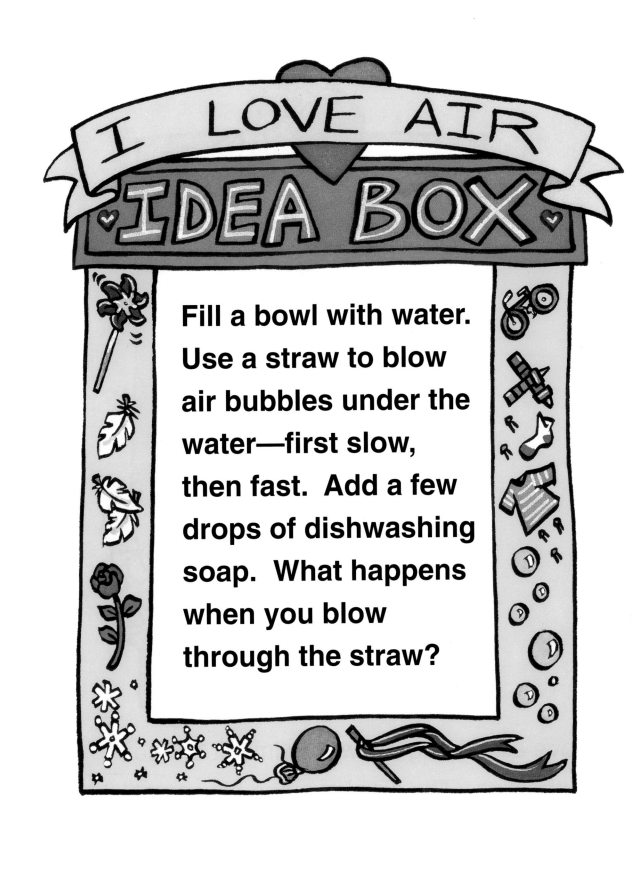

# I LOVE AIR
## IDEA BOX

Fill a bowl with water. Use a straw to blow air bubbles under the water—first slow, then fast. Add a few drops of dishwashing soap. What happens when you blow through the straw?

I love air.  I hang my wet swimsuit on the clothesline.  The air blows and blows until it is dry.  Now my suit is ready to wear again tomorrow.  I love air.

# I LOVE AIR

## IDEA BOX

Instead of putting laundry in a clothes dryer, hang it outside. The air does a good job of drying clothes...and makes them smell good, too.

I love air.  Dad and I ride our bikes to the country.  We stop just to breathe.  The air smells clean.  I love air.

# I LOVE AIR

## IDEA BOX

Find a blank piece of paper. On one side, draw a world with clean air. On the other side, draw a world with dirty air. What makes air dirty? How can people keep air clean?

I love air.  Clean air is good for all living things—
like you and me.   I love clean air.

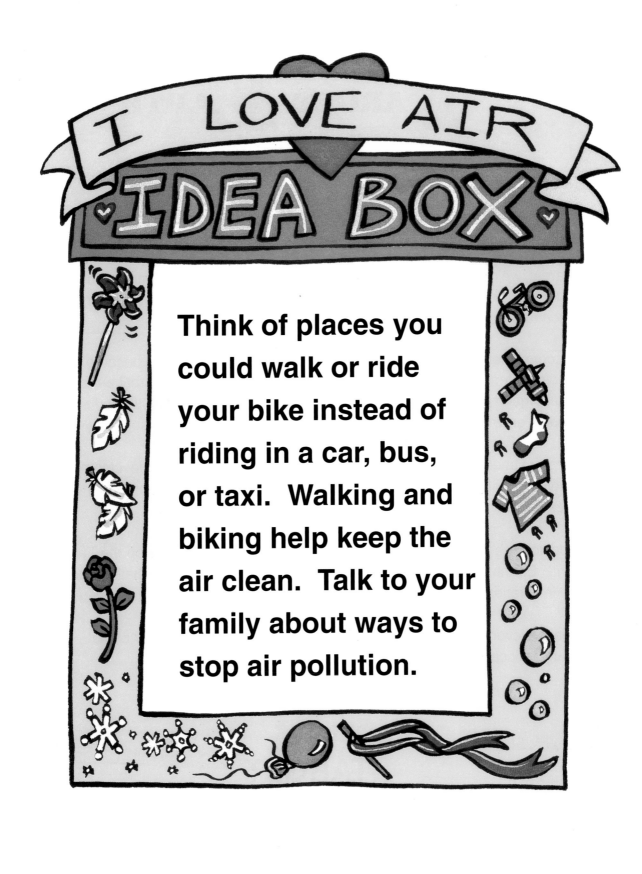

I LOVE AIR

IDEA BOX

Think of places you could walk or ride your bike instead of riding in a car, bus, or taxi. Walking and biking help keep the air clean. Talk to your family about ways to stop air pollution.

# TARGET EARTH™ COMMITMENT

At Target, we're committed to the environment. We show this commitment not only through our own internal efforts but also through the programs we sponsor in the communities where we do business.

Our commitment to children and the environment began when we became the Founding International Sponsor for Kids for Saving Earth, a non-profit environmental organization for kids. We helped launch the program in 1989 and supported its growth to three-quarters of a million club members in just three years.

Our commitment to children's environmental education led to the development of an environmental curriculum called Target Earth™, aimed at getting kids involved in their education and in their world.

In addition, we worked with Abdo & Daughters Publishing to develop the Target Earth™ Earthmobile, an environmental science library on wheels that can be used in libraries, or rolled from classroom to classroom.

Target believes that the children are our future and the future of our planet. Through education, they will save the world!

**TARGET.**

Minneapolis-based Target Stores is an upscale discount department store chain of 517 stores in 33 states coast-to-coast, and is the largest division of Dayton Hudson Corporation, one of the nation's leading retailers.